D1586681

5/may/71 (8)

DAGGERS OF THE THIRD GERMAN REICH

1933-1945

ANDREW MOLLO

A Historical Research Unit publication
Copyright 1967 by Historical Research Unit
27, Emperor's Gate
London, S.W.7, England

Drawings by Malcolm McGregor
Printed by Stanwill Press Ltd., London, S.E.14

Price 50s

INTRODUCTION

This pamphlet is not an attempt to list every known type of German dagger, nor have I tried to describe the many variations that existed in the size, detail, and finish of each model. What I have set out to do, is to form a reliable basis for further research into the subject.

I would like to thank Mr Ivor F. Bush, Mr Eric Campion, Mr Brewster Cross, and Mr René Johnson for their permission to illustrate daggers from their collections, and particularly my old friends James Joslyn, and Colonel C. M. Dodkins, C.B.E., D.S.O., Retd., for their enthusiastic assistance in the compilation of this work.

Andrew Mollo,

London, 1967.

INDEX**Page**

TERMINOLOGY

REGULATION DAGGER or VORSCHRIFTSMÄSSIGER DOLCH

Worn with regulation uniform as specified in the appropriate dress regulations. These weapons conformed exactly to the sealed pattern (Probe) deposited in the main clothing office (Bekleidungsamt) of each service or organisation. They were either issued by the state or purchased from an authorised retailer.

PRIVATELY PURCHASED DAGGER or EXTRADOLCH

These weapons could be worn with undress uniforms only, and were expected to conform externally to the regulation pattern. No limit was placed on the quality of manufacture or on the ornamentation of the blade.

HONOUR DAGGER or EHRENDOLCH

Awarded by leaders of the Armed forces, NSDAP, and other organsiations as a personal award in recognition of the loyalty or long service of the recipient. Most honour daggers conformed basically to the regulation pattern whilst those awarded to very important persons were often specially designed.

1 HEERES OFFIZIERDOLCH
Army Officer's Dagger

Introduced on the 4th May, 1935 for all officers, generals, medical and veterinary officers, musicians and officials with officer's rank.

Dagger Old silver sheath, pommel and crossguard. Yellow horn or white plastic grip. Overall length 40 cms.

Hanger Two field grey velvet straps on which was sewn aluminium braid.

White metal fittings for officers, gilt for generals.

Knot Standard aluminium knot with long cord.

Ref Uniformen-Markt, 1935, No. 6, p. 2.

Uniformen-Markt., 1939, No. 6, p. 319.

Dr. Klietmann, Die Deutsche Wehrmacht 1934-1945, Sheet No. 34.

2 EHRENDOLCH DES HEERES
Honour Dagger of the Army

Presented to STABSCHEF DER SA. VIKTOR LUTZE on the 28th December, 1940, on the occasion of his fiftieth birthday by GENERAL-FELDMARSCHALL VON BRAUCHITSCH on behalf of the German army.

Dagger Old silver sheath, pommel and cross-guard. White ivory grip bound with silver wire. Damasc steel blade with raised gilt inscription "Das Deutsche Heer dem Stabschef Lutze 28.12.1940". On the reverse "Treue um Treue". Overall length 46 cms.

Hanger A central shield covered in scarlet cloth on which is embroidered in aluminium wire the Wehrmacht eagle. From the top and two bottom edges of the shield are attached the field-grey cloth covered carrying straps on which are embroidered in aluminium wire, bars and oakleaves. The background to the oakleaves is scarlet edged in grey silk thread. The metal clips on the ends of the two bottom straps are thought to be replacements.

Knot Standard aluminium knot with long cord.

Ref Actual dagger in the collection of Mr. Ivor F. Bush.

"Die SA.", 1940, No. 3, p. 16.

Uniformen-Markt, 1941, No. 2, p. 14.

Note For Army Forestry Service see section on State Forestry Service.

German officer in walking out dress, Paris, 1940

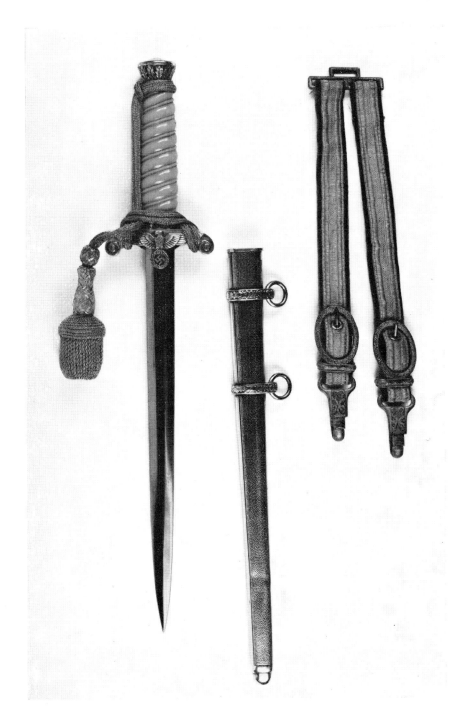

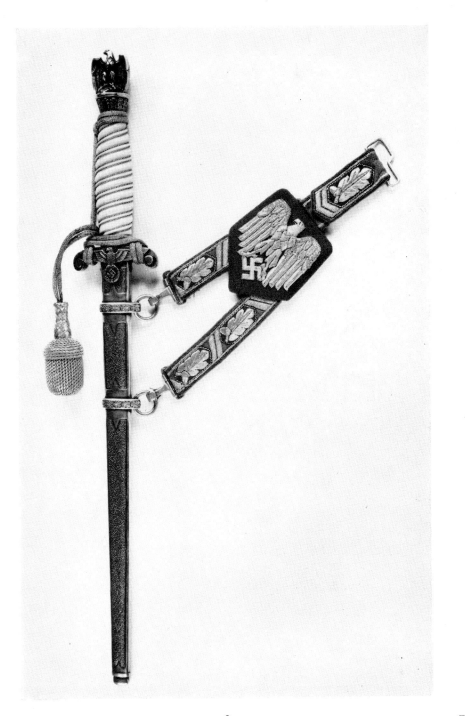

1

2

DEVELOPMENT OF THE NAVAL OFFICERS' DAGGER

The naval officer's dagger as worn during the Third Reich was a development of the Imperial German naval dagger first introduced in 1849.

In 1901 a dagger was introduced for naval officers which had, up to that time, been worn by cadets only. The dagger had a gilt metal sheath with two carrying rings, a gilt metal cross-guard, yellow horn grip and a pommel in the shape of the German imperial crown.

On the 28th November, 1918 a new flame shaped pommel was introduced, as well as a black grip and black metal sheath, with one carrying ring.

On the 5th June, 1919 the black grip and sheath were officially discarded and the old gilt metal sheath with two carrying rings, and yellow horn grip were re-introduced.

On the 28th April, 1938 the 'Flammenkopf' was replaced by the Wehrmacht eagle.

Ref Dr. Phil. Wolfgang Janke (Marinebekleidungsamt Kiel) Originalbeitrag für den Uniformen-Markt, 1939, No. 14, p. 221-222.

3 MARINE OFFIZIER DOLCH
Naval Officer's Dagger

Introduced in its final form on the 20th April, 1938 for all commissioned ranks from PORTEPEEUNTEROFFIZIER upwards, as well as FÄHN-RICHE and KADETTEN.

Dagger Gilt etched or hammered sheath, pommel and cross-guard. White or yellow horn or plastic grip, bound with gilt wire. Officers who received their commissions before the 1st November, 1918 were entitled to wear the imperial naval dagger with crown pommel. Many variations of the naval dagger appear, both in the detail on the blades and on the pattern of sheath, especially in the mountings for the carrying rings. Blades were either plain or etched with naval scenes and motifs. Overall length 36 cms.

Hanger Two black moire straps on black or dark blue velvet base with gilt metal fittings. Administrative officials with officers rank had white metal fittings.

Knot Standard aluminium knot with long cord.

4 EHRENDOLCH DER KRIEGSMARINE
Honour Dagger of the Navy

Introduced in 1938 by GENERALADMIRAL Dr. H. C. RAEDER as an award for exceptional merit. It was not originally intended as an award for bravery in war. Six honour daggers were presented between 1938 and 1942.

Dagger Gilt metal sheath, pommel and cross-guard. White ivory grip bound with gilt metal oakleaves. The swastika in the pommel was decorated with brilliants. The blade was damasc steel and bore a personal inscription to the recipient and Raeder's signature in raised gilt letters. Overall length 42 cms.

Hanger Same as for standard pattern dagger.

Knot Standard aluminium knot with long cord.

Ref Uniformen-Markt, 1938, No. 4, p. 50.

Uniformen-Markt, 1939, No. 14, p. 221.

Dr. Klietmann. Die Deutsche Wehrmacht 1934-1945, Sheet No. 4.

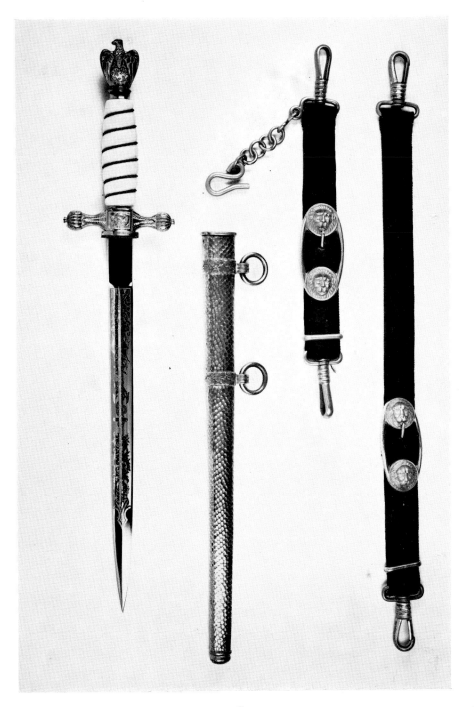

3

5 LUFTWAFFE FLIEGERDOLCH

Air Force Pilot's Dagger

Introduced in 1935 for officers, PORTEPEEUNTEROFFIZIERE and FÄHNRICHE. After the introduction in October, 1937 of a new officer's dagger, the old 'Fliegerdolch' was only to be worn by flying personnel up to the completion of their training, and by FÄHNRICHE etc., awaiting their commission. Officers were not allowed to continue wearing the 'Fliegerdolch' unless it had been presented to them for a specific reason.

Dagger Light blue leather covered sheath and grip. Nickel-plated or white metal sheath and hilt fittings. Grip bound in silver wire. Gilt swastika in pommel and cross-guard. Overall length 48 cms.

Hanger Two chains of different lengths made up of linked white metal rings.

Knot Standard aluminium knot with short cord.

Ref Uniformen-Markt, 1935, No. 7, p. 5.
    Uniformen-Markt, 1938, No. 13, p. 196.

6 LUFTWAFFE OFFIZIERDOLCH

Air Force Officer's Dagger

Introduced on the 1st October, 1937 for all officers, officials with officer's rank, members of the Air Force engineer's corps, and officers of the SA. Regiment "STANDARTE FELDHERRNHALLE" when wearing Air Force uniform. On the 12th March, 1940 PORTEPEEUNTEROFFIZIERE were also entitled to wear the dagger.

Dagger Grey metal sheath and hilt pieces. Gilt swastika on pommel. Yellow horn or white plastic grip bound with twisted silver wire.

Hanger Two grey velvet straps on which was sewn grey braid with an aluminium stripe down each side. Grey metal fittings.

Knot Standard aluminium knot with short cord.

Ref Uniformen-Markt, 1937, No. 16, p. 243.
    Uniformen-Markt, 1940, No. 12, p. 91.
    Der SA. Mann, 1938.

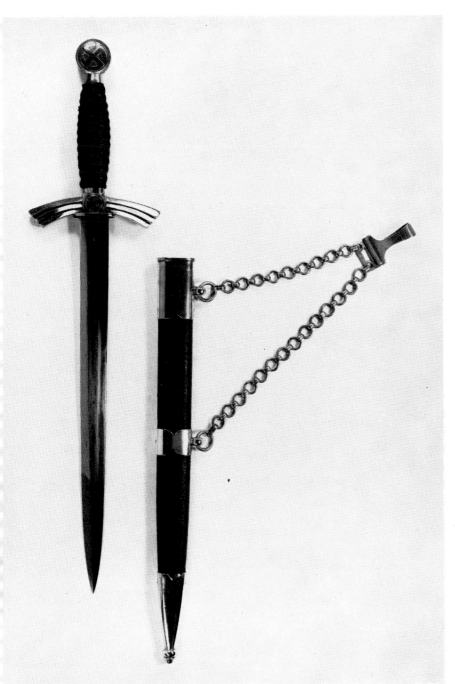

5

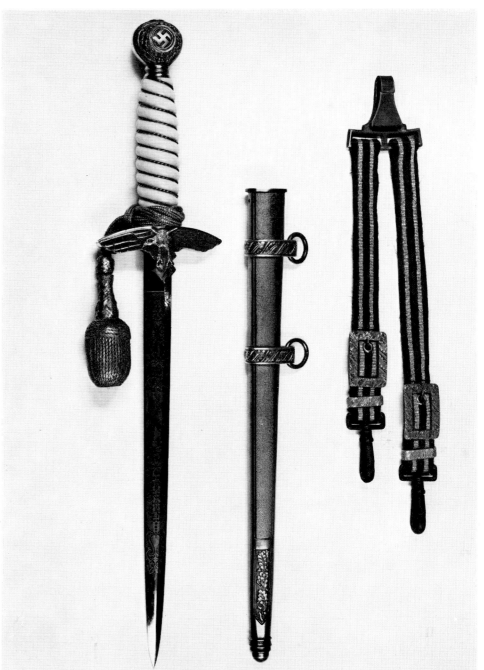

6

7 REICHSMARSCHALL DOLCH

Reichs-Marshal's Dagger

Designed to be worn with Reichs Marshal's uniform, and made by students of the Berlin Technical Academy.

Dagger Gilt metal sheath, cross-guard and pommel. Pommel and cross-guard set with rubies and diamonds. White ivory fluted grip. An iron cross engraved on the top surface of the cross-guard on both sides of the grip.

Hanger White velvet straps on which was sewn aluminium braid with a gold stripe down each side. Gilt metal fittings.

Knot Standard aluminium knot with short cord.

Ref Illustrated London News. Saturday, November 24, 1945, p. 685.
Uniformen-Markt, 1940, No. 22, p. 175.

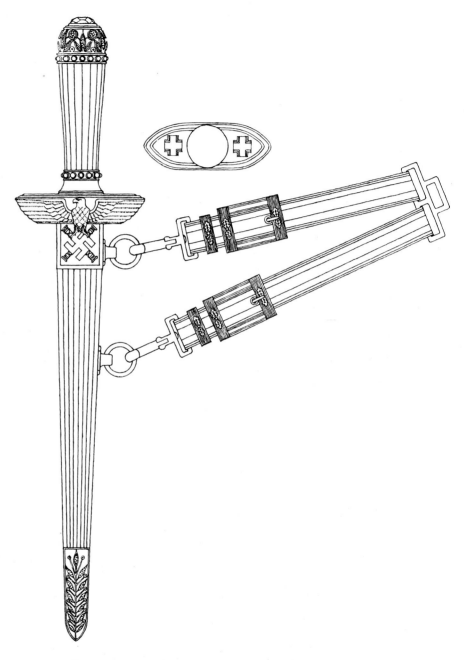

7

8 SA.-DIENSTDOLCH MODELL 1933

SA Service Dagger Model 1933

Introduced on the 15th December, 1933 for all ranks in the SA and Naval SA (SA.-MARINE), to be worn with all orders of dress.

Dagger Brown wooden grip with inset white metal eagle and enamel SA badge. Nickel-plated sheath and hilt pieces. Brown metal sheath. Etched motto on blade ALLES FÜR DEUTSCHLAND. Overall length 37 cms.

Hanger See page 50

Ref Das Sponton. Zur Geschichte des SA und SS Dolches, 1963, No. 13/14, p. 92.

Freiheer von Eelking. Uniformen der Braunhemden. Zentral Verlag der NSDAP, Munich, 1934, p. 22.

9 SA.-EHRENDOLCH MODELL 1933

SA Honour Dagger Model 1933

Established by SA order of the 3rd February, 1934, it entitled 125,960 SA men, who had been members of the SA or Hitler Youth prior to the 31st December, 1931 to have the inscription IN HERZLICHER FREUNDSCHAFT ERNST RÖHM etched on the blades of their 1933 model daggers. After Röhm's assassination, an SA order dated the 1st July, 1934 ordered the inscription to be erased.

10 HÖHERE SA.-FUHRER EHRENDOLCH MODELL 1933

High-Ranking SA Leader's Honour Dagger Model 1933

Awarded by the OBERSTEN SA.-FÜHRUNG in recognition of loyalty, long service and other exceptional deeds.

Dagger Similar to the standard 1933 model but with gilt metal hilt and sheath pieces. The hilt pieces were often finely chiselled. The sheath fittings had a groove along the outer edges. The blades were either standard or made of damasc steel with the motto in raised gilt letters with gilt oakleaves at each end of the motto. Overall length 37 cms.

Ref Eickhorn Kundendienst, Ausstattung mit Seitenwaffen bei den Parteiformationen. Carl Eickhorn, Solingen.

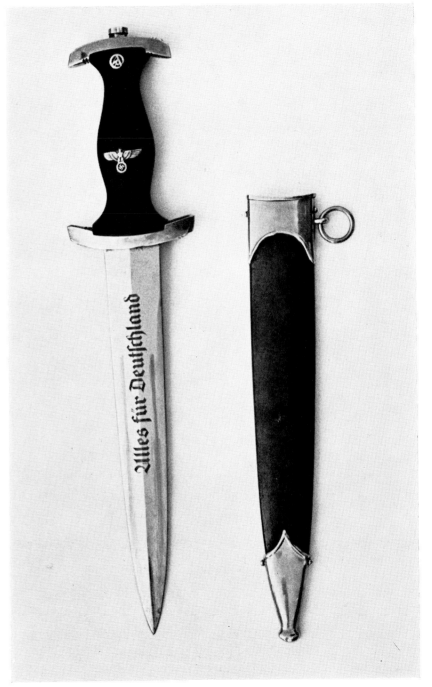

8

11 VICTOR LUTZE'S SA HONOUR DAGGER

This is one of two special SA honour daggers worn by STABSCHEF DER SA. VIKTOR LUTZE.

Dagger Brown wooden grip with inset gilt-metal eagle and enamel SA badge. Gilt-metal sheath and hilt pieces. Gilt-metal chain. Dark-brown polished leather sheath. Damasc steel blade with the motto in raised gilt letters with gilt oakleaves at each end of the motto. The whole dagger is longer and narrower than the standard SA dagger. Overall length 42 cms.

Ref Actual dagger in the collection of Mr. Ivor F. Bush.

12 VICTOR LUTZE'S SA HONOUR DAGGER (MODEL 1937)

Presented to STABSCHEF DER SA VIKTOR LUTZE on the 28th December, 1937 on the occasion of his forty-seventh birthday by GRUPPENFÜHRER REIMANN on behalf of the officer corps of the SA.-STANDARTE-FELDHERRNHALLE.

Dagger Gilt sheath and hilt pieces. Brown wooden grip. Blade of damasc steel, with on one side the SA motto, in raised gilt letters, and on the other in raised gilt gothic script, IHREM STABSCHEF IM ALTEN SA.-GEIST ZUM 28.12.37 DAS FÜHRERKORPS DER STANDARTE FELDHERRNHALLE. Overall length 45 cms.

Hanger Two brown velvet straps of different lengths on which was sewn brown braid, with a steel grey stripe down each side. Gilt metal fittings.

Ref Actual dagger in the collection of Mr. Eric Campion.

13 SA.-FÜHRERDOLCH MODELL 1937

SA Leader's Dagger Model 1937

This dagger was described in the SA newspaper "Der SA Mann" as the new SA dagger. Worn in any number for the first, time, by members of Lutze's staff when he visited Rome in July 1938.

Dagger Old-silver sheath and hilt pieces. Brown plastic grip. Etched motto on blade ALLES FÜR DEUTSCHLAND. Overall length 45 cms.

Hanger Two brown velvet straps of different lengths on which was sewn brown braid with a steel-grey stripe down each side. White metal fittings.

Ref Actual example was in the collection of Mr. John Scott.
Der SA Mann. Kampfblatt der Obersten SA.-Führung der NSDAP 1938, No. 47, p. 4.

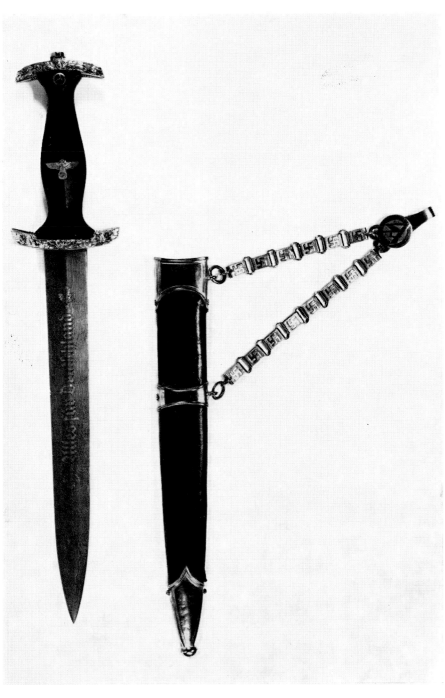

11

STABSCHEF DER SA. VIKTOR LUTZE wearing another pattern of SA honour
dagger. Planet News photo.

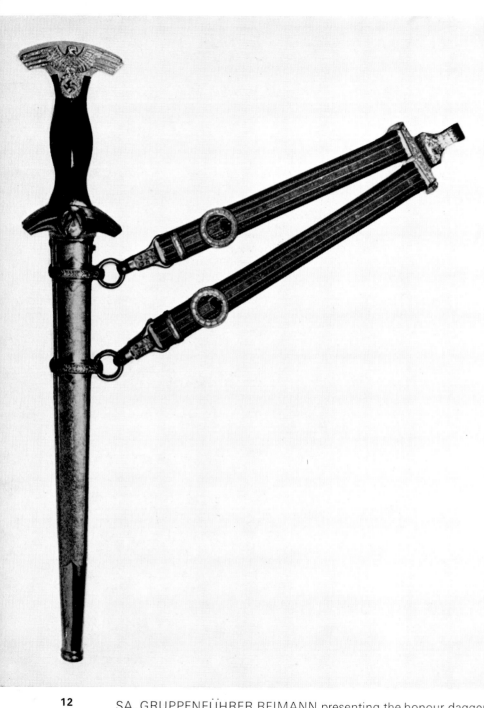

12 SA. GRUPPENFÜHRER REIMANN presenting the honour dagger to STABSCHEF DER SA. VIKTOR LUTZE, on behalf of the officer's corps of the SA. - STANDARTE FELDHERRNHALLE.

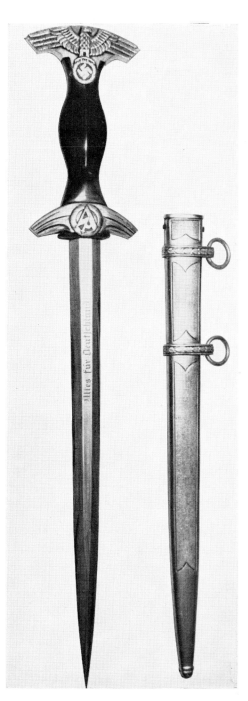

13

VIKTOR LUTZE and his staff with COUNT CIANO, Rome, 1938. Luce photo.

14 NSKK.-DIENSTDOLCH MODELL 1933
NSKK Service Dagger Model 1933

Introduced on the 15th December, 1933 for all ranks in the NSKK and Naval NSKK (NSKK.-MARINE). It was worn with all orders of dress.

Dagger Brown wooden grip with inset white metal eagle and enamel SA badge. Nickel-plated hilt and sheath fittings for NSKK, copper coloured gilt for Naval NSKK. Black metal sheath. Etched motto on blade ALLES FÜR DEUTSCHLAND. Overall length 37 cms.

Hanger See page 50

15 HÖHERE NSKK.-FÜHRER EHRENDOLCH MODELL 1933
High-ranking NSKK Leader's Honour Dagger Model 1933

Awarded by the NSKK.-KORPSFÜHRUNG in recognition of loyalty, long service and other exceptional deeds.

Dagger Similar to the standard 1933 model but with finely chiselled silver coloured hilt pieces. The nickel-plated sheath fittings were either etched or had a groove along the outer edges. The blades were either standard or made of damasc steel with the motto in raised gilt letters with gilt oakleaves at each end of the motto. Overall length 37 cms.

Hanger See page 50

16 NSKK.-DIENSTDOLCH MODELL 1936
NSKK Service Dagger Model 1936

Introduced in 1936 for all ranks in the NSKK and Naval NSKK to be worn with undress uniforms only.

Dagger Brown wooden grip with inset white metal eagle and enamel SA badge. Nickel-plated hilt and sheath fittings and chain for NSKK, copper coloured fittings for Naval NSKK. Etched motto on blade ALLES FÜR DEUTSCHLAND. Overall length 37 cms.

Ref Der Reichsorganisationsleiter der NSDAP. Organisationsbuch der NSDAP. Munich 1943, p. 407 and plate 43.

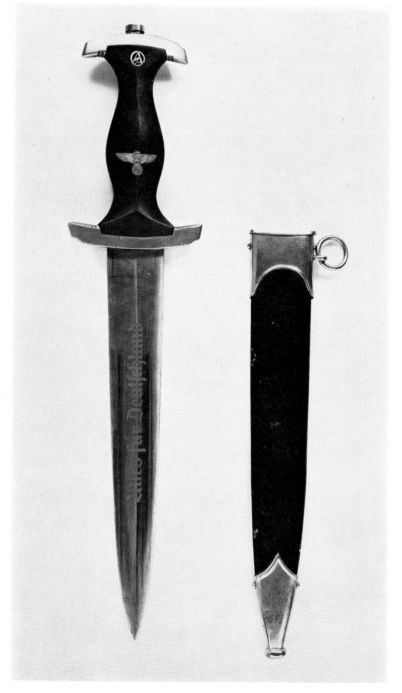

15

16

HITLER, GOEBBELS and NSKK.-KORPSFÜHRER HÜHNLEIN at the opening of the 1938 German Motor Show in Berlin.   Hulton Picture Library.

17 SS.—DIENSTDOLCH MODELL 1933
SS Service Dagger Model 1933

Introduced on the 15th December, 1933 for all ranks in the ALLGEMEINE-SS. It was worn with all orders of dress.

Dagger Black wooden grip with inset white metal eagle and enamel SS badge. Nickel-plated sheath and hilt pieces. Black metal sheath. Etched motto on blade MEINE EHRE HEISST TREUE. Overall length 37 cms.

Hanger See page 50

18 SS.—EHRENDOLCH MODELN 1933 UND 1934
SS Honour Daggers Models 1933 and 1934

SS order of the 22nd February, 1934, entitled 9,900 SS men, who had been members of the SA, SS or Hitler-Youth prior to the 31st December, 1931, to have the inscription IN HERZLICHER FREUNDSCHAFT ERNST RÖHM etched on the blades of their daggers. After Röhm's assassination an SS order dated the 4th July, 1934 ordered the inscription to be erased.

On Tuesday the 3rd July, 1934 after Röhm and his supporters had been liquidated, an action in which the SS took no small part, Himmler presented 200 SS men with an honour dagger bearing his signature, in recognition of their faithful service during the crisis. The inscription may have been IN HERZLICHER FREUNDSCHAFT H. HIMMLER which is found on the blades of SS daggers.

19 SS.—DIENSTDOLCH MODELL 1936
SS Service Dagger Model 1936

Introduced on the 25th August, 1936 for all ranks in the SS, to be worn with undress uniforms only.

Dagger Identical to the 1933 model with the exception of an extra sheath fitting and a chain hanger.

Knot Standard aluminium knot with long cord.

Ref Der Reichsorganisationsleiter der NSDAP Organisationsbuch der NSDAP. Munich, 1943. pp. 431 to 433 and plate 51.
Elizabeth Wiskemann. History Today. Vol XIV No. 6, June 1964, p. 380.
Uniformen-Markt. 1944, No. 6, p. 8, with illustration.

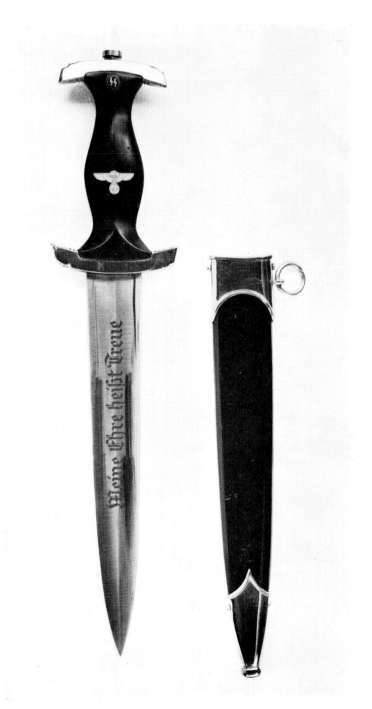

17

SS-GRUPPENFÜHRER UND REFERENT LOEPER wearing 1933 model dagger.

SS.-OBERSCHARFÜHRER HEINRICH ROGOWSKI with 1936 model dagger, July 1937. W. Bloomer photo.

19

20 HJ.-FAHRTENMESSER
Hitler-Youth knife
Worn by all ranks up to OBERSCHARFÜHRER with all orders of dress.

Dagger Black bakelite grip with inset enamel Hitler-Youth badge, Nickel-plated pommel, back-plate and cross-guard. Black metal sheath. Engraved motto on blade BLUT UND EHRE. Overall length 27 cms.

Hanger Black leather loop riveted to sheath.

21 DJ.-FAHRTENMESSER
German-Youth knife
Worn by members of the DEUTSCHES JUNGVOLK IN DER HITLER-JUGEND up to the age of fourteen when they joined the Hitler-Youth.

Dagger Black bakelite grip. Aluminium pommel, back-plate and cross-guard. Black metal sheath with applied Hitler-Youth badge in enamel. The knife in its sheath weighed only 120 grms. Overall length 20 cms.

Hanger Black leather loop riveted to sheath.

22 HJ.-EHRENFAHRTENMESSER
Hitler-Youth Honour knife
Awarded for outstanding feats of sport and leadership.

Dagger Black bakelite grip. Hitler-Youth badge was etched on pommel and surrounded with oakleaves. On some models the Hitler-Youth badge was replaced by the Hitler-Youth flag or a plain swastika within a circle. The motto on the blade was etched within a surround of oakleaves. Overall length 27 cms.

Hanger Black leather loop riveted to sheath.

23 HJ.-FÜHRERDOLCH
Hitler-Youth Leader's Dagger
Introduced in 1938 for leaders with the rank of GEFOLGSCHAFTFÜHRER to STABSFÜHRER.

Dagger Silver wire bound grip. White metal pommel on the top of which in relief was the Hitler-Youth badge. White metal cross-guard and sheath pieces. Etched motto on blade BLUT UND EHRE. Overall length 35 cms.

Hanger Two black leather straps with plain white metal fittings.

Ref Der Organisationsleiter der NSDAP. Organisationsbuch der NSDAP. Munich 1943. Plate 61/63 with three illustrations.

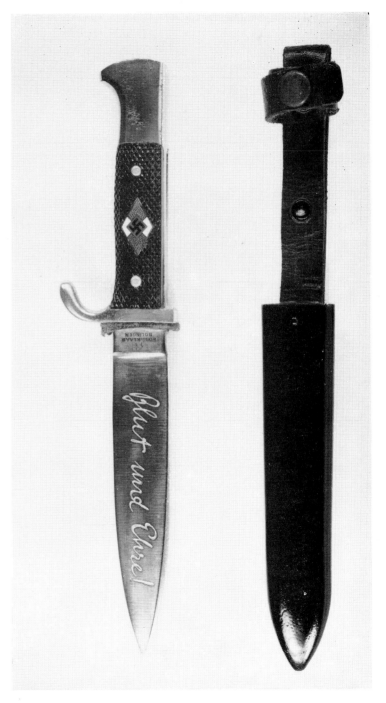

20

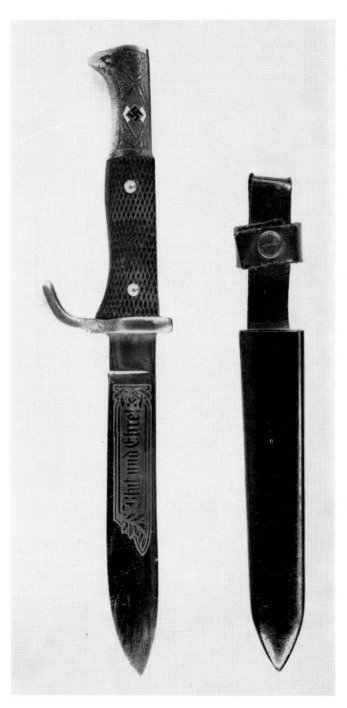

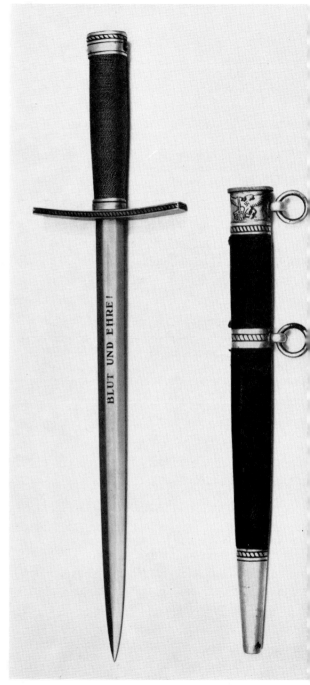

24   **21**   **22**   **23**

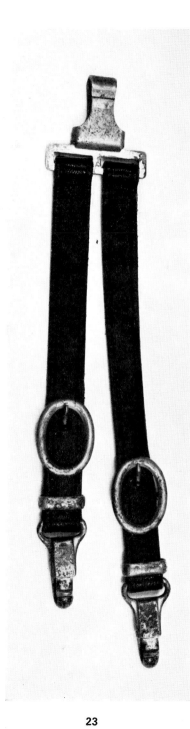

REICHSJUGENDFÜHRER ARTHUR AXMANN inaugurates Hitler-Youth banners at a parade in Prague, in November 1940. Heinrich Hoffman photo.

24 NPEA.-KURZTEILNEHMER DIENSTDOLCH

NPEA Student's Dagger

Worn by JUNGMANNEN DER OBERSTUFE with Hitler-Youth, and the special uniform National Political Education Institute.

Dagger Plain light brown wooden grip. Nickel-plated hilt pieces, the top one of which sometimes bore the name of the institution. Khaki coloured bayonet pattern sheath. Etched motto on blade MEHR SEIN ALS SCHEINEN. Overall length 37 cms.

Hanger Brown leather bayonet pattern frog (Tasche).

25 NPEA.-LEITER DIENTSTDOLCH

NPEA Staff Dagger

Identical to the 1933 SA model, it was probably introduced for instructors and the permanent staff of the political institutes.

Dagger Light brown wooden grip both with and without the inset white metal eagle. Nickel-plated sheath and hilt pieces. Khaki coloured sheath. Etched motto on blade MEHR SEIN ALSO SCHEINEN Overall length 37 cms.

Hanger See page. 50

26 NPEA.-LEITER DIENSTDOLCH MODELL 1936

NPEA Staff Dagger Model 1936

Probably introduced in 1936 for instructors and permanent staff of the political institutes.

Dagger Light brown wooden grip both with and without the inset white metal eagle. Nickel-plated sheath and hilt pieces. The two sheath fittings indicate that the dagger was worn with chains, but no reference to, or illustration of them, has so far been found. Etched motto on the blade MEHR SEIN ALS SCHEINEN. Overall length 37 cms.

Ref Uniformen-Markt 1940, No. 5, p. 33.

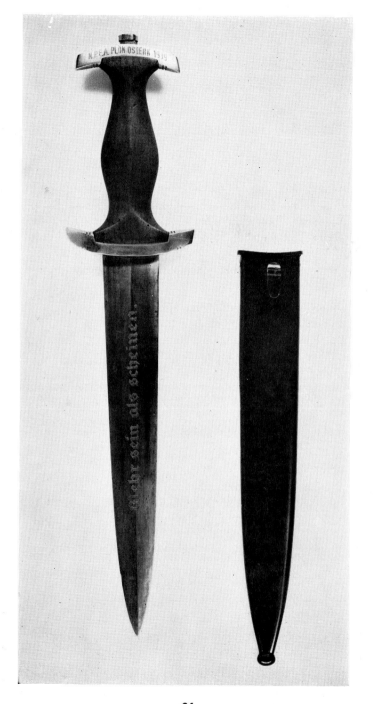

24

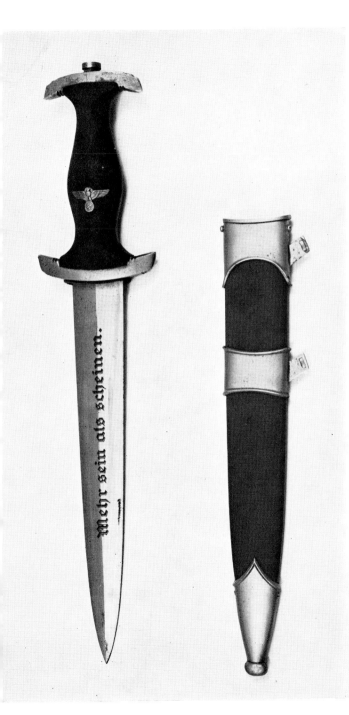

Hitler-Youth parade in the Old Town Square, Prague in November 1940. Hugh Page-Taylor Collection.

27 RAD.-HAUMESSER

RAD Dagger

Introduced in 1936 for all Labour Service leaders from FELDMEISTER upwards. In 1937 a new dagger was introduced for RAD leaders and the old pattern was, from then on, worn by TRUPPFÜHRER to UNTER-FELDMEISTER only.

Dagger Stag-horn grip. Nickel-plated pommel, back-plate, cross-guard, and sheath pieces. Black metal sheath. Etched motto on blade ARBEIT ADELT. Overall length 40 cms.

Hanger Special brown leather straps with nickel-plated clips.

28 RAD.-HAUMESSER MODELL 1937

RAD Leader's Dagger Model 1937

Introduced in 1937 for leaders from FELDMEISTER and AMTSWALTER to REICHSARBEITSFÜHRER to replace the old dagger.

Dagger White plastic grip. White metal pommel, back-plate, cross-guard, and sheath. Etched motto on blade ARBEIT ADELT. Overall length 40 cms.

Hanger Two light brown leather straps with white metal fittings. GENERALARBEITSFÜHRER upwards had gilt-metal fittings.

Ref Uniformen-Markt 1938. No. 5, p. 77.

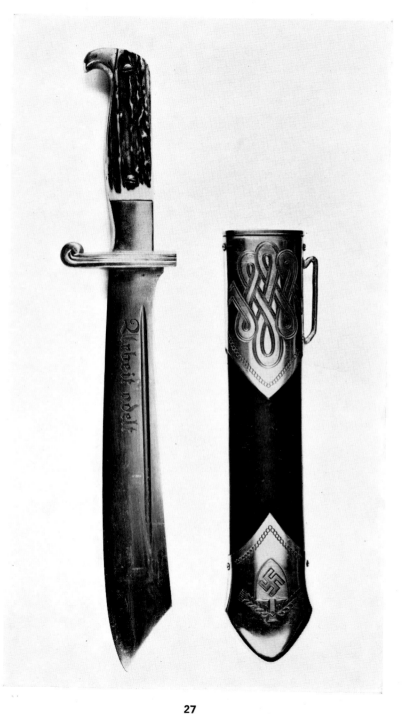

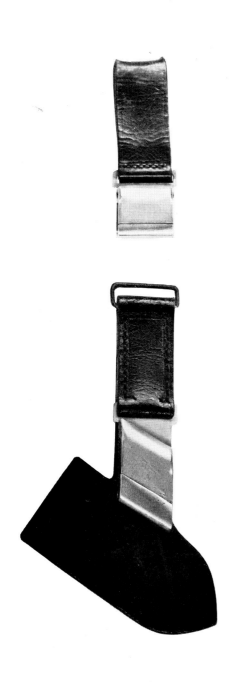

27

28

REICHSARBEITSFÜHRER CONSTANTIN HIERL addressing a rally of the Dutch Labour Service in Den Haag, May 1942. Wiener Library.

29 NSFK.—FLIEGERMESSER
NSFK. Pilot's Knife
Introduced in 1934 for all ranks in the NSFK.

Dagger Light blue leather covered grip and sheath. Nickel-plated pommel and cross-guard into which was set a black enamel swastika. White metal sheath fittings. Overall length 33 cms.

Hanger Light blue leather strap attached permanently to the carrying ring on the top sheath fitting.

Ref Uniformen-Markt 1937. No. 19, p. 296.

30 WASSERSCHUTZPOLIZEI OFFIZIERDOLCH
Water Police Officer's Dagger
Worn by officers and inspectors of the Water Police until April 1939, when they were supposed to have been presented or issued with, the SS-Police sword.

Dagger Black or dark blue leather covered grip bound in gilt wire. On some daggers a gilt metal police badge was applied to the grip. Gilt metal pommel, cross-guard, and sheath. Blades were often etched with naval motifs. Overall length 36 cms.

Hanger Identical to Naval Officer's.

Ref Uniformen-Markt 1939. Nos. 4 and 18, pp. 52 and 280.

31 FEUERWEHR OFFIZIERDOLCH
Fire Service Officer's Dagger
Worn by officers of the Volunteer (FREIWILLIGE FEUERWEHR) and the Professional Fire Service (BERUFSFEUERWEHR) with the rank of BRANDMEISTER upwards. With the introduction of new uniforms for the whole German police and fire services in May 1936, the dagger was replaced by the SS-Police sword.

Dagger Black-leather covered grip with nickel-plated pommel, cross-guard and sheath pieces. Black leather sheath. Blades were often etched with firefighting motifs. Overall length 48 cms.

Hanger Black leather straps with plain nickel-plated fittings.

Ref Eickhorn Kundendienst, Ausstattung mit seitenwaffen bei der Feuerwehren. Carl Eickhorn, Solingen.

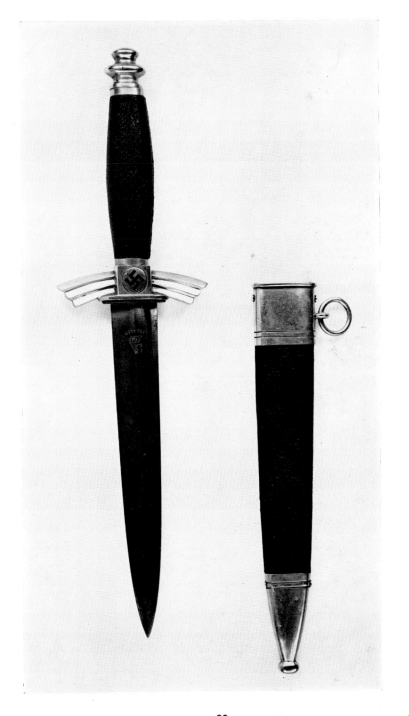

29

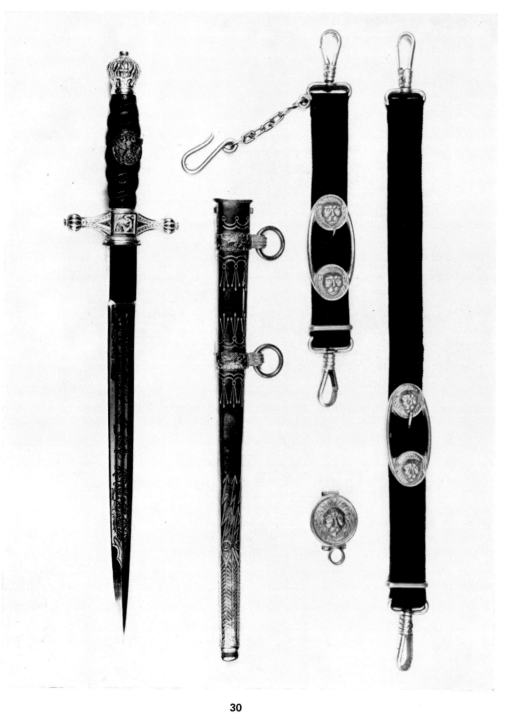

30

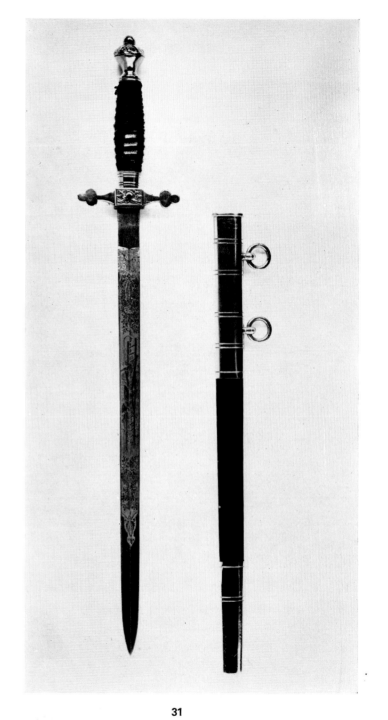

32 RLB Dolch

RLB Dagger

Introduced in 1935 for all ranks from TRUPPMANN to OBERTRUPP-MEISTER.

Dagger Nickel-plated pommel and cross-guard. Black wooden grip with applied white metal star with RLB and a swastika in prussian blue enamel. In 1938 the letters were changed to a prussian blue swastika. Black metal sheath with nickel-plated fittings. Overall length 36 cms.

Hanger Black leather strap riveted to the carrying ring.

33 RLB.—FÜHRERDOLCH

RLB Leader's Dagger

Introduced in 1935 for RLB leaders with the rank of LUFTSCHUTZ-FÜHRER to PRÄSIDENT DES REICHSLUFTSCHUTZBUND.

Dagger Nickel-plated pommel and cross-guard. Black leather covered grip with applied white metal star with RLB and a swastika in prussian blue enamel. Black leather covered sheath with nickel-plated fittings. Overall length 40 cms.

Hanger Black leather strap riveted to the carrying ring.

34 RLB.—FÜHRERDOLCH MODELL 1938

RLB Leader's Dagger Model 1938

Introduced in 1938 to replace the old RLB leader's dagger.

Dagger Nickel-plated pommel and cross-guard. Black leather covered grip with applied white metal star with swastika in prussian blue enamel. Black leather covered sheath with nickel-plated fittings. Overall length 39 cms.

Hanger Two prussian blue leather straps with white metal fittings.

Ref Uniformen-Markt, 1935, No. 2, p. 5.

Uniformen-Markt, 1938, No. 18, p. 277.

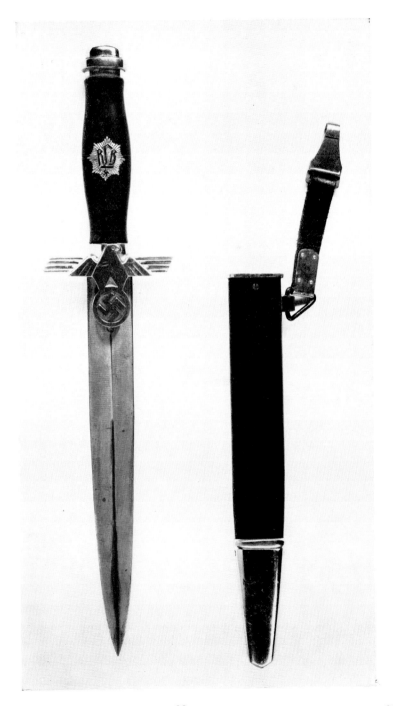

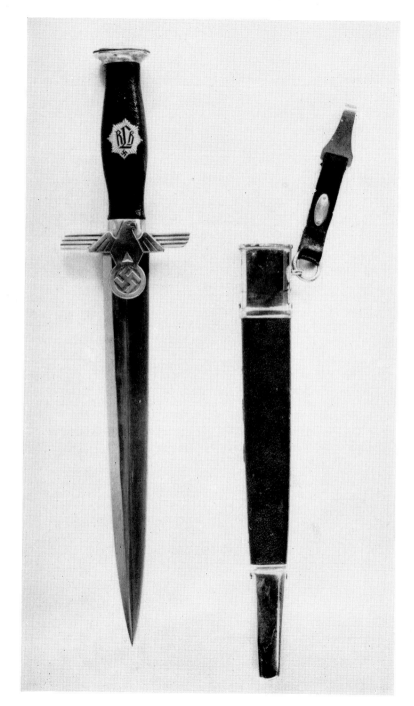

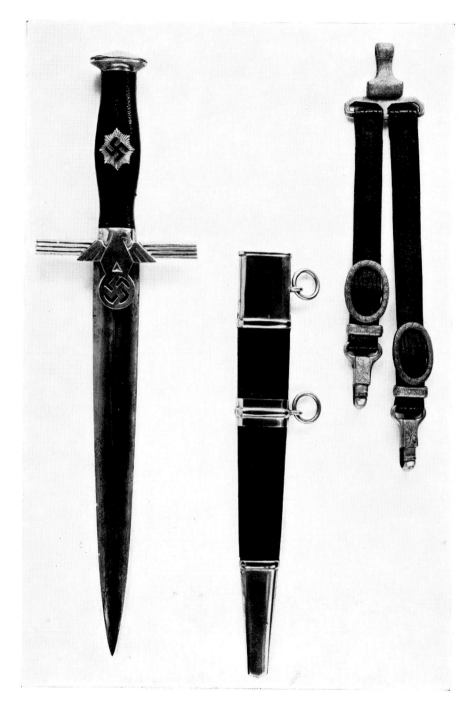

33

35 TN.—FÜHRERDOLCH

TN Leader's Dagger

Introduced on the 30th November, 1938 for all TN leaders from KAMERADSCHAFTSFÜHRER to CHEF DER TN.

Dagger Old silver pommel, cross-guard and sheath. Yellow plastic grip. The TN emblem was etched on the reverse of the blade under the cross-guard. Overall length 43 cms.

Hanger Two patterns existed. Two plain black leather straps or two black velvet straps on which was sewn black braid with an aluminium stripe down each side. White metal fittings. LANDESFÜHRER to CHEF DER TN had gilt metal fittings.

Knot Standard aluminium knot with short cord.

36 TN.—HAUER

TN Knife

Introduced on the 30th November, 1938 for all ranks from NOTHELFER to HAUPTSCHARFÜHRER.

Dagger Nickel-plated pommel and cross-guard. White plastic grip. Black metal sheath with nickel-plated fittings. The TN emblem was etched on the reverse of the blade under the cross-guard. Overall length 40 cms.

Hanger Black leather frog attached permanently or clipped to the top sheath fitting.

Knot See page 48

Ref Uniformen-Markt 1938, No. 24, p. 381.
　　　Uniformen-Markt 1940, No. 12, p. 92.

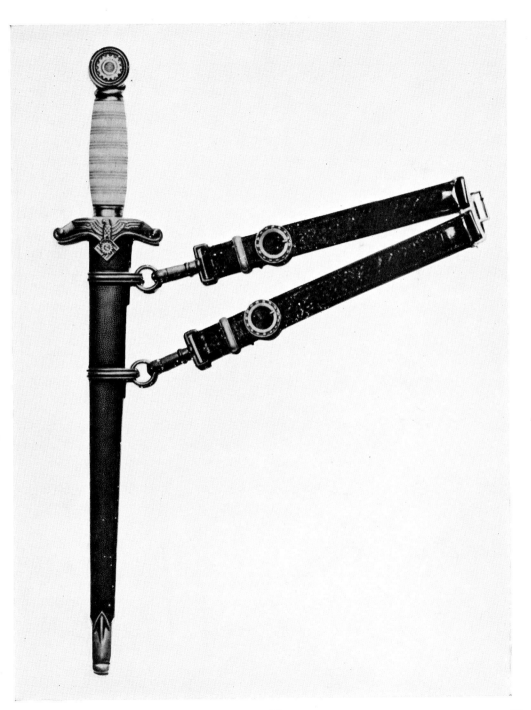

36

36

37 LANDZOLLBEAMTEN DOLCH
Land Customs Official's Dagger

Introduced in August 1937 to replace the sword for all officials of the Ministry of Finance, with the rank of OBERZOLLSEKRETÄR upwards, as well as those with the rank of ZOLLPRAKTIKANT.

Dagger White metal pommel and cross-guard. Green leather covered grip bound in silver wire. Green leather covered sheath with white metal fittings. Overall length 41 cms.

Hanger Two dark green velvet straps on which was sewn aluminium braid with a dark green stripe down each side. White metal fittings. OBERFINANZPRÄSIDENT to REICHSMINISTER DER FINANZEN had gilt metal fittings.

Knot See page 48

38 WASSERZOLLBEAMTEN DOLCH
Water Customs Official's Dagger

Introduced in August 1937 for Water Customs officials with the rank of MASCHINENBETRIEBSLEITER to ZOLLAMTMANN.

Dagger Gilt metal pommel and cross-guard. Dark blue leather covered grip bound in gilt wire. Dark blue leather covered sheath with gilt metal fittings. Overall length 41 cms.

Hanger Black moire straps on black or dark green velvet base with white metal fittings. OBERFINANZPRÄSIDENT to REICHSMINISTER DER FINANZEN had gilt metal fittings.

Knot Standard aluminium knot with long cord.

Ref Uniformen-Markt 1937. No. 17, pp 268 with illustrations.
Bekleidungsvorschrift für Reichsfinanzverwaltung. Amtsblatt der Reichsfinanzverwaltung, No. 19, Berlin 14th August, 1937. p. 103.

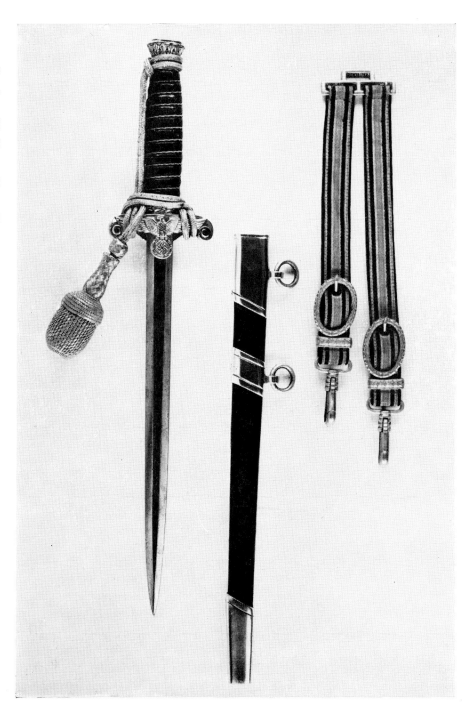

39 REICHSBAHN FÜHRERDOLCH
Railway Leader's Dagger

Worn by officials of the REICHSBAHN DIREKTION BERLIN with the rank of OBERZUGFÜHRER upwards.

Dagger Gilt metal pommel, cross-guard and sheath. Black plastic grip. Overall length 41 cms.

Hanger Dark blue velvet base on which was sewn gilt braid with a dark blue line down each side. Plain-gilt metal fittings.

Ref Drawing made from an illustration that appeared in the trade paper 'Wehr und Spaten'. Date of publication unknown.

40 REICHSBAHN-WASSERSCHUTZPOLIZEI FÜHRERDOLCH
Railway Water Police Leader's Dagger

Dagger Gilt metal pommel, cross-guard and sheath. Black plastic grip. Overall length 41 cms.

Hanger Dark blue velvet base on which was sewn gilt braid with a dark blue stripe down each side. Gilt army pattern fittings.

Ref Eickhorn Kundendienst, Ausstattung mit Seitenwaffen beim Bahn-schutz. Carl Eickhorn, Solingen.

41 BAHNSCHUTZ FÜHRERDOLCH
Railway Protection Service Leader's Dagger

Dagger White-metal pommel, cross-guard and sheath. Black plastic grip. Overall length 41 cms.

Hanger Black velvet base on which was sewn aluminium braid with a black stripe down each side. White metal fittings.

Knot See page 49

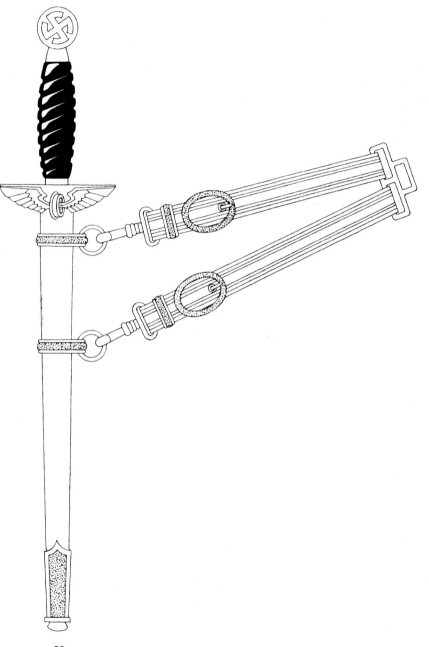

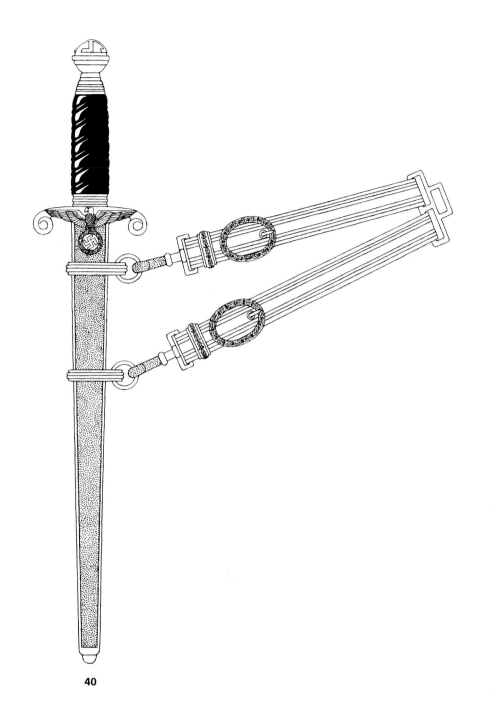

40

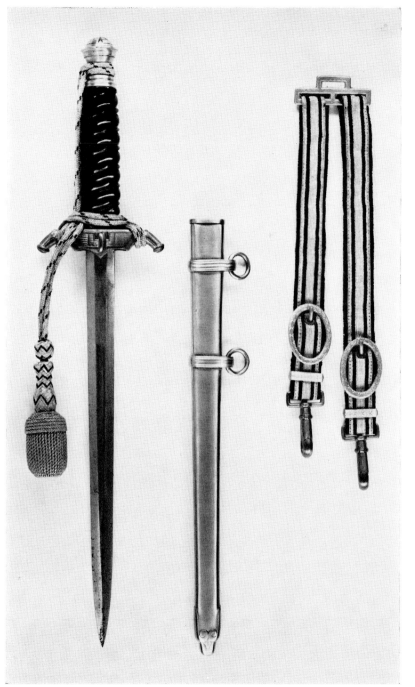

41

42 POSTSCHUTZ FÜHRERDOLCH

Postal Protection Service Leader's Dagger

Worn by officials with the rank of ZUGFÜHRER upwards.

Dagger Nickel-plated pommel and cross-guard with inset black enamel swastika. Black wooden grip with applied Postal Service badge in white metal. Black metal sheath with nickel-plated fittings and chains. Overall length. 40 cms.

Knot See page 49

Ref Uniformen-Markt 1939. No. 3, p. 44.

43 POSTSCHUTZ DOLCH

Postal Protection Service Dagger

Worn by officials up to the rank of ZUGFÜHRER.

Dagger Nickel-plated pommel and cross-guard with inset black enamel swastika. Black wooden grip with applied white-metal Postal Service badge. Overall length. 36 cms.

Hanger Black leather strap riveted to the carrying ring.

44 DRK.—FÜHRERDOLCH

German Red Cross Leader's Dagger

Introduced in 1938 for all officials with the rank of WACHTFÜHRER upwards.

Dagger White metal pommel, cross-guard and sheath. Yellow or white plastic grip. Overall length 38 cms.

Hanger Two buff coloured velvet straps on which were sewn buff coloured braid with an aluminium stripe edged in red down each side. White metal fittings.

45 DRK.—HAUER

German Red Cross Knife

Introduced in 1938 for Red Cross men with the rank of HELFER to HAUPTHELFER.

Dagger Nickel-plated pommel and cross-guard. Black plastic grip. Black metal sheath and nickel-plated fittings. Overall length 40 cms.

Hanger Black leather bayonet frog (Seitengerättasche).

Ref Uniformen-Markt, 1938. No. 4, p. 53.

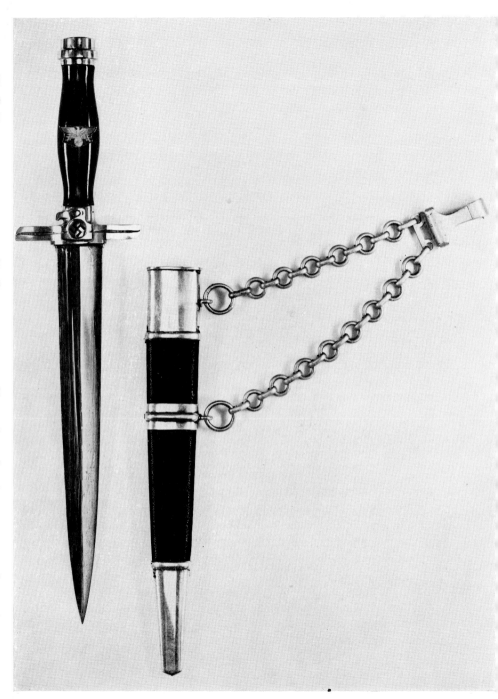

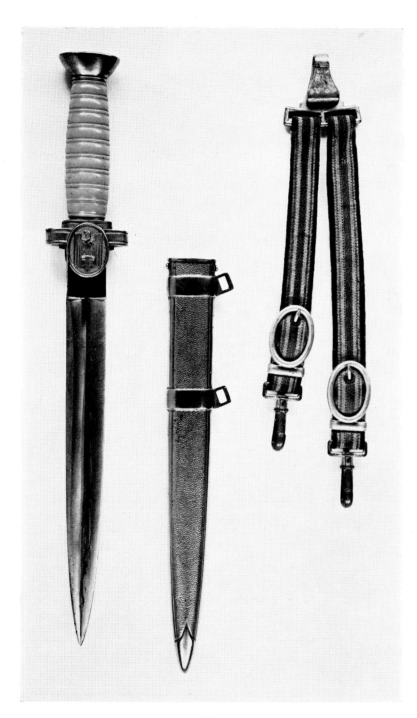

44

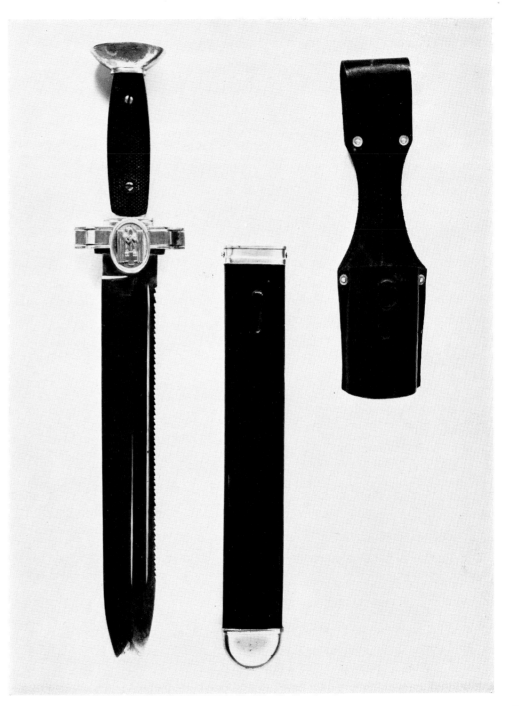

45

46 STAATSBEAMTE DOLCH
State Official's Dagger
Introduced on the 30th March, 1939 for all Reichs and State authorities and their staffs.

Dagger Old-silver pommel, cross-guard, back-plate, and sheath. Mother-of-pearl grips. Overall length 39 cms.

Hanger Grey velvet straps on which was sewn aluminium braid with a grey stripe down each side. Grey metal fittings.

Knot Small size aluminium knot with long cord.

Ref Uniformen-Markt, 1939. pp. 132 and 325.

47 FISCHEREIAUFSICHTSBEAMTE DOLCH
Fishery Control Officials's Dagger
Introduced in 1940, to replace the naval officer's sword, for high-ranking officials only.

Dagger Identical to the state official's dagger but with black sheath.

Hanger Not known.

Knot Not known.

Ref Uniformen-Markt 1940, p. 146.

48 OSTBEAMTE DOLCH
Eastern Official's Dagger
In 1941 a dagger was projected for officials of the Ministry of Occupied Eastern Territories. It was to have been identical to the State Official's, but gilt, with gilt braid hangers. A year later, a completely new uniform was introduced which included a dagger, the design of which was to be withheld until the end of the war. It is not known which of these two patterns was in fact worn.

Dagger White metal pommel, cross-guard and sheath. White plastic grip. Overall length 41 cms.

Hanger Aluminium braid on brown velvet base with white-metal fittings.

Knot Small size aluminium knot with long cord.

Ref Uniformen-Markt, 1941. No. 19, p. 196.

Uniformen-Markt, 1942. No. 15, p. 113

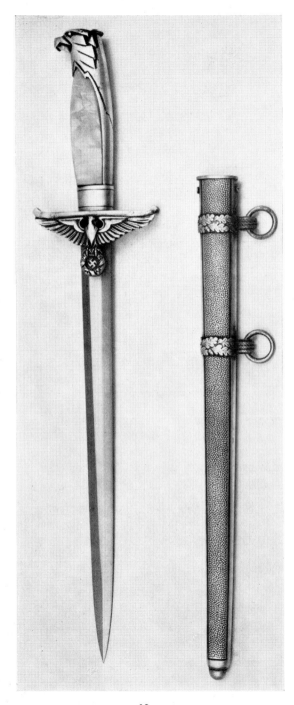

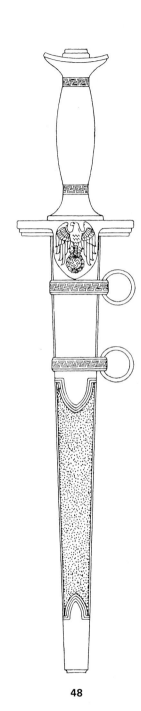

48

REICHSLEITER ROSENBURG (right) and GAULEITER KOCH (5th from right) during a tour of the Ukraine in June 1943 This photograph proves conclusively that one of the two versions of the Eastern Official's dagger was worn. Heinrich Hoffman photo.

49 DIPLOMATEN DOLCH
Diplomat's Dagger

Worn for the first time by members of the Diplomatic Corps during Hitler's visit to Rome in May, 1938.

Dagger Old-silver pommel, back-plate, cross-guard and sheath. Mother-of-pearl grips. Overall length 39 cms.

Hanger Black velvet base on which was sewn aluminium braid. White metal fittings.

Knot Small size aluminium knot with long cord.

Ref Uniformen-Markt 1938. No. 11, p. 167.

50 STAATSFORSTDIENST HIRSCHFÄNGER
State Forestry Service Cutlass

Many variations of the State Forestry Service cutlass were worn by both the general (GEMEINDE FORSTDIENST) and private (PRIVAT FORST-DIENST) forestry services. The Army and Air Force Forestry services used the simpler and less ornate model with scallop-shell guard. The basic difference between the commissioned and non-commissioned ranks' cutlasses was the grip. FÖRSTER upwards had ivory or white stag-horn grips, whereas ANWÄRTER and FÖRSTAUFSEHER to UNTERFÖRSTER had brown stag-horn grips.

Cutlass Chiselled gilt metal guard and shell. White ivory or brown stag-horn grips with applied gilt metal oakleaves and acorns. Blued blades were often finely etched with hunting scenes. Black leather sheath with gilt metal fittings. Average overall length 31 cms.

Hanger Black leather frog.

Knot See page 49

Ref Dienstbekleidungsvorschrift für den Staats, Gemeinde und Privat-
forstdienst vom 22. April 1938. Berlin 1938.
Uniformen-Markt 1938, p. 183-184.
Uniformen-Markt 1941, p. 63.

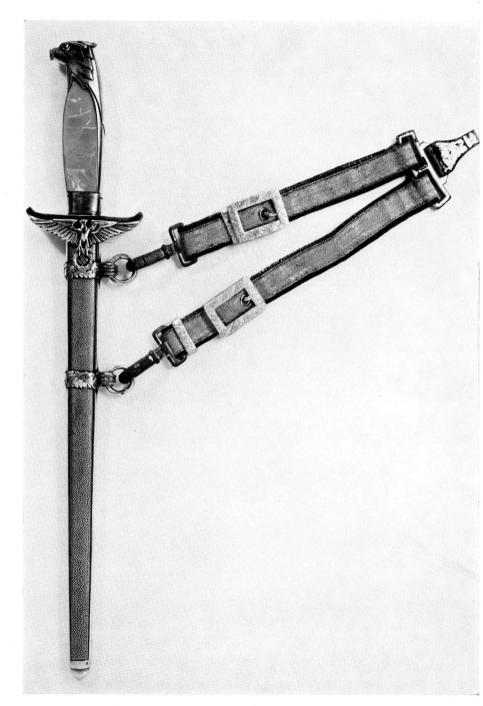

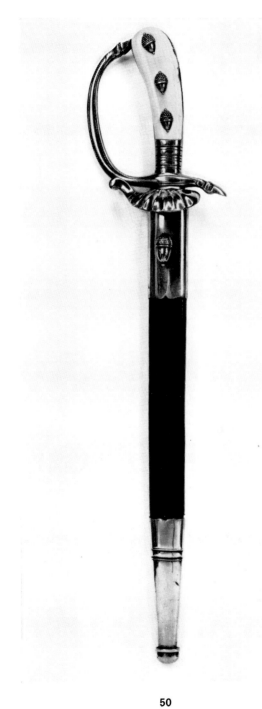

50

50

51 DEUTSCHE JÄGERSCHAFT HIRSCHFÄNGER
German Hunter's Association Cutlass

All members of the association were entitled to wear, as from the 22nd March, 1936, either a regulation or an 'extra' cutlass. Only professional hunters (BERUFSJÄGER) were allowed to wear it with a knot.

Cutlass Nickel-plated pommel, cross-guard and shell. Stag-horn grip with applied association badge in white-metal. Blades were often etched with hunting scenes and motifs. Green leather sheath with nickel-plated fittings. Overall length 49 cms.

Hanger Green leather frog.

Knot Introduced on the 29th January, 1937 for all professional hunters with the exception of apprentice. See page 49

Ref Uniformen-Markt, 1936. No. 7, p. 108.

52 DEUTSCHER SCHÜTZENVERBAND HIRSCHFÄNGER
German Rifle Association Cutlass

Introduced in 1939 for members of the association for wear with uniform only.

Cutlass Nickel-plated pommel, cross-guard and shell. White wooden grip with applied gilt metal crossed rifles. Association badge in black enamel mounted on the shell. Blade etched with appropriate motifs. Black leather sheath with nickel-plated fittings. Overall length 54 cms.

Hanger Black leather frog.

Knot See page 49

Ref Uniformen-Markt, 1939. No. 5, p. 73.

HM 1943, Nr 468. EINSTELLUNG DER FERTIGUNG VON BLANKEN SEITENWAFFEN.
ORDER DISCONTINUING THE MANUFACTURE OF EDGED WEAPONS

The Reichs-Minister for Armament and Munitions has ordered the discontinuation of the manufacture of sabres, swords, and daggers. Those who provide their own uniforms and who do not possess such weapons will wear a pistol on their belt on all occasions where such arms are required. See order H.V.B1.1941, teil B,Nr.226.

O. K. H. (Ch.H.Rüst u.BdE)

27.5.43.—64a 10.12—Abt.Bkl. (IIIa).

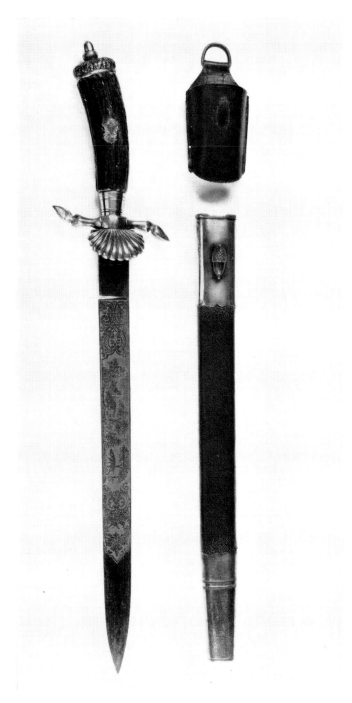

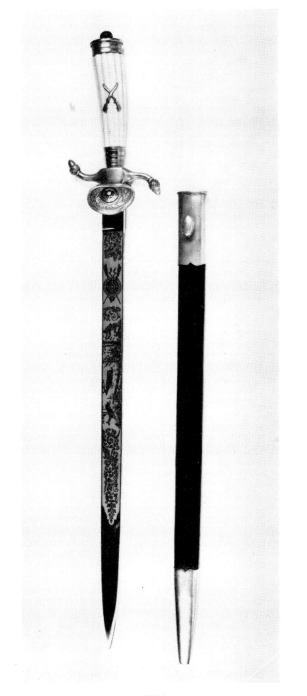

51

52

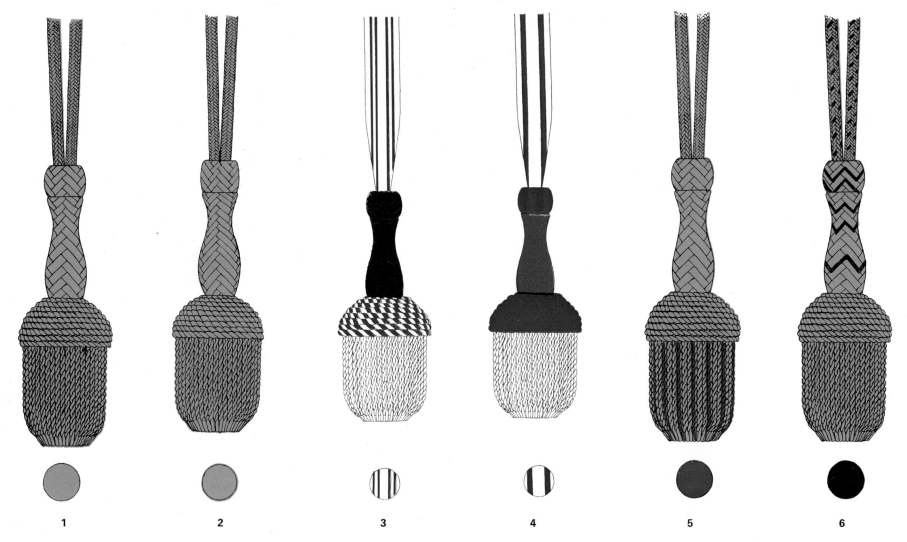

KNOTS

1 Standard aluminium knot with 42 centimetre long cord, was worn by officers of the Army, Navy, and by commissioned ranks in the SS, Water Police, and Customs.

Standard aluminium knot with short 23 centimetre long cord, was worn by Air Force officers and by leaders of the Technical Emergency Service

2 Small version of the standard aluminium knot with long cord was worn by State Officials, Diplomats and Eastern Officials with officer's rank.

3 Knot for Technical Emergency Service non-commissioned leaders on air raid service (LUFTSCHUTZDIENST).

4 Knot for Technical Emergency Service men on stand-by service (BEREITSCHAFTDIENST).

Other Technical Emergency Service colours worn by non-commissioned leaders and men on their knots, were green for general service (ALLGEMEINER DIENST) and blue for technical service (TECHNISCHEDIENST).

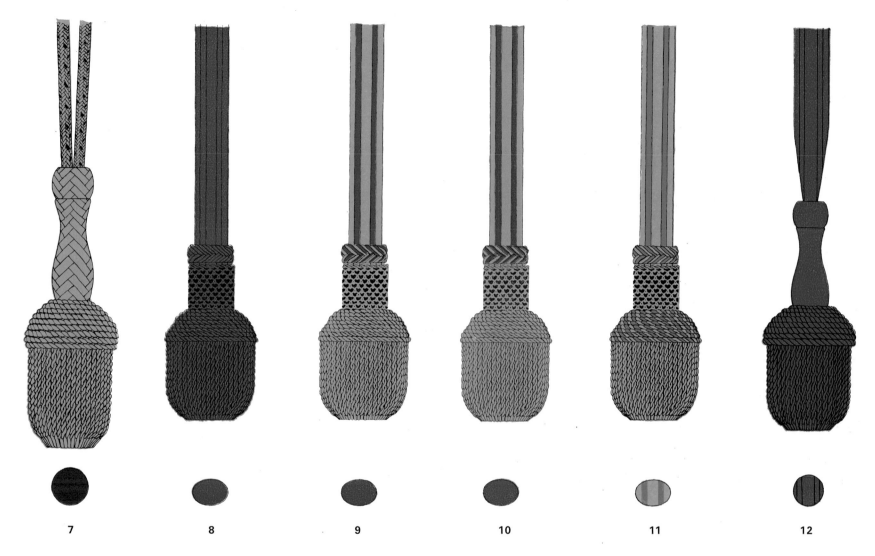

7   8   9   10   11   12

5   Knot for customs officials with the rank of ZOLLSEKRETÄR and OBERZOLLSCHIFFER.

6   Knot for Railway Protection Service (BAHNSCHUTZ) leaders.

7   Knot for Postal Protection Service Leaders with the rank of ZUGFÜHRER upwards.

8   Knot for forestry officials with the rank of FORSTANWÄRTER upwards.

9   Knot for forestry officials with the rank of FÖRSTER upwards.

10   Knot for forestry officials with the rank of OBERLANDFÖRSTER.

11   Knot for professional Hunters (BERUFSJÄGER) in the German Hunter's Association.

12   Knot for members of the German Rifle Association.

GENERAL NOTE

All officials who had held commissions in the armed forces were allowed to wear the standard aluminium knot instead of the pattern specified for their organisation.

THE WEARING OF DAGGERS

ARMY The dagger was worn instead of the sword, bayonet or pistol with the following orders of dress

UNDRESS UNIFORM	KLEINER DIENSTANZUG
REPORTING DRESS	MELDUNGANZUG
WALKING-OUT DRESS	AUSGEHANZUG

When wearing a tunic, a special belt was worn over the right shoulder or round the waist, under the tunic. The belt had an aluminium hook to which the top of the dagger was attached. When the overcoat was worn, the same clip was then passed through a slit under the left pocket flap. The top of the hanger was then covered by the pocket flap.

NAVY The Navy had a special dagger-belt (Dolchkoppel) to which the two carrying straps were attached. The braid belt (Scharpe) also had two rings on the inside to which the two carrying straps could be attached. The dagger could be worn with either of these belts, depending on the order of dress. On board ship with :—

PARADE DRESS (WARTIME)	GROSSER DIENSTANZUG
SERVICE DRESS	DIENSTANZUG
DAY DRESS	TAGES DIENSTANZUG
MESS DRESS	MESSE ANZUG

On land with :—

PARADE DRESS	GROSSER DIENSTANZUG
DAY DRESS	TAGESDIENSTANZUG
MESS DRESS	MESSEANZUG

In peace-time the dagger-belt was worn over the frock-coat (Rock) and under the reefer (Jackett), except by PORTEPEEUNTEROFFIZIEREN who wore the dagger-belt over the reefer. On certain occasions the dagger was worn with the braid-belt instead of the sword with parade dress. With mess dress the dagger-belt was always worn under the waistcoat. With overcoat and cape the method of wearing the dagger was optional.

Cadets always wore the dagger-belt under their tunic.

Coastal units wearing field-grey service uniform wore the dagger in a black leather bayonet frog from the service belt. In 1942 they were ordered to wear the dagger in the same way as in the Army.

AIR FORCE Daggers were worn in the same way and with the same orders of dress as in the Army. Air Force non-commissioned officers who were entitled to wear the 'Fliegerdolch' with undress uniform wore it from a ring on their brown leather service belts. With walking-out dress and gala uniform, when the belt was not worn, the dagger was carried from a belt worn under the tunic.

PARTY FORMATIONS

The 1933 model daggers of the SA., Naval SA., NSKK., Naval NSKK., SS., and NPEA., were worn with one of two basic types of straps.

Type 1 FESTELLRIEMEN was a short brown or black leather strap with an oval nickel-plated buckle at one end and a nickel-plated clip at the other. The strap was buckled on the ring on the sheath and then clipped onto a ring worn on the Service belt.

Type 1a As type 1 but with an extra leather strap that fastened around the top of the grip and prevented the dagger from swinging violently.

Type 2 DOLCHTRAGTASCHE used when the dagger was worn with entrenching tool or full equipment. Many different patterns existed.

Type 2a One of the many variations of type 2.

With service and walking-out dress the dagger was worn with types 1 and 1a.

With field-service dress (GROSSER DIENSTANZUG) the dagger was worn with types 2 and 2a.

The 1936 model daggers of the above organisations with chains were worn with service dress from a ring on the service belt. With undress uniforms when the belt was not worn, the dagger was attached to a clip underneath the left side pocket flap. The 1936 model dagger was not worn with field-service dress.

OTHER ORGANISATIONS

All other organisations who had daggers with either leather or braid hangers, wore them from a belt under the tunic, or from a clip under the left side pocket flap. With service dress and in winter, when the overcoat was worn, the daggers were sometimes worn from a ring on the service belt.

Generally speaking the dagger of any organisation was not worn on active service nor on such activities as skiing or flying. Daggers, pistols and swords were never worn together.

1 1a 2 2a

BIBLIOGRAPHY

Der Reichsorganisationsleiter der NSDAP. Organisationsbuch der NSDAP, Munich 1934-1943.

Dr. Klietmann. Die Deutsche Wehrmacht 1934-1945. "Die Ordensammlung", Berlin 1961.

Carl Eickhorn. Eickhorn Kundendienst. Solingen 1939.

Friedrich Schirmer und Fritz Weiner. Feldgrau Mitteilungsblätter einer Arbeitsgemeinschaft. Celle 1953-1967.

Uniformen-Markt. Fachzeitung der gesamten Uniformen-, Effekten-, Fahnen-, Paramenten-, Orden-, und Ehrenzeichen fur Heer und Marine, Wehr und Sportverband. Berlin 1934-1945.

Eberhard Hettler. Uniformen der Deutschen Wehrmacht, Berlin, 1938.

Eberhard Hettler. Nachtrag 1939/40 zu Uniformen der Deutschen Wehrmacht. Berlin, 1940.

Freiheer von Eelking. Uniformen der Braunhemden. Zentral Verlag der NSDAP, Munich 1934.

James P. Attwood. The Daggers and Edged Weapons of Hitler's Germany. Privately published, Berlin, 1965.

Daggers of the German Third Reich. Z.M. Military research Co. New York, 1958.

Nazi Daggers and Dress Bayonets an illustrated reference. R and L Enterprises. Ohio, U.S.A., 1959.